How Much Do You REALLY Know About The Love Of Your Life

A couples quiz to see how much you really know about each other and your relationship

Cheryl Pryor

Arlington & Amelia

Copyright © 2017 Cheryl Pryor

Arlington & Amelia Publishers

ArlingtonAmeliaPub@cfl.rr.com

First Printing

ISBN:10-1-886541-17-5
ISBN:13-978-1-886541-17-7

FOR THE LOVE OF MY LIFE

TABLE OF CONTENTS

About This Book

Ladies First

Now It's His Turn

About This Book

Who this book is for: This book is for those who are in a loving relationship that want to see how much they know about their mate, helpmate, loved one, spouse, whatever you call your significant other; and to open lines of communication to learn more about what makes their loved one tick.

If you're looking for a fun way to see how much you really know about the love of your life this book is a fun and entertaining way to do so. The way the book is designed is she fills in her answers in the first part of the book. He answers duplicate questions in the back part of the book. You can then compare your answers and see how you did.

Break it down to a category at a time and it will last you over a month if you filled it out every single day. It's a great conversation starter for the two of you. Use it nights when there's nothing on TV, while you're on the road, or sitting in an airport waiting for a flight, or just when you want to make some time to spend together.

In this day of social media where we tell the world everything about ourselves, take this couples quiz to see how well we communicate and listen to the one we love.

You will find your memory and your knowledge tested on just how much you *really* know about each other while having a great time. This book keeps it light and entertaining while at the same time asks some pretty challenging questions. It's meant to enhance your relationship, not to start any arguments. Take this time to listen and see just how much you *really* know about the one you love.

Ladies First

Ladies fill out the first part of the book and your loved one
will fill out the second half

In The Beginning

1. What is the name of the hospital where he was born

_____

2. How much did he weigh when he was born

_____

3. Was he born in the morning or the evening

_____

4. In what city was he born

_____

5. What is his birthdate – including the year

_____

6. What day of the week was he born

_____

7. What is his middle name

_____

8. What was his favorite toy as a child

_____

9. Did you grow up in the same city and state he did

_____

10. What is his astrological sign

_____

School Days

1. What do you remember of a school memory he told you about

_____

_____

2. Where did he attend elementary school

_____

3. What was his favorite subject in school

_____

4. What was his least favorite subject

_____

5. Where did he attend high school...name of school

_____

6. What was his major in college

7. What is the most embarrassing thing he did in his school days

_____

_____

8. Was there a teacher that inspired or influenced him in any way

_____

9. His most memorable teacher (good or bad) was

_____

10. He went to college with the intention of pursuing what career

_____

3

When You Met

1. How did you meet each other:

   A. work

   B. through a friend

   C. social media

   D. out and about / intrduced ourselves

2. Where did you meet

   _____

3. What was your first impression of him

   _____

4. What did you find you had in common when you first met

   _____

5. Do you remember what you talked about the first time

you met

_____

6. When he asked you for your phone number/text/email address/to friend you on facebook; what was your first thought:

A. give him the info

B. give him a wrong number/email address

C. hope he would contact you ASAP

7. Did you initially hope he would contact you again after the first day/night you met

_____

8. What was the first positive trait about him that made you think perhaps this was meant to be

_____

9. After your friends met him, what was their advice to you

_____

10. After your parents met him, what was their advice to you

_____

4

First Time For Everything

1. Where did you go on your first date?

_____

2. Where were you when you first kissed?

_____

3. Who called/texted/ or emailed who first

_____

4. Who said I love you first?

_____

5. What is the first gift he bought for you?

_____

6. How long did you know him before you first met his family

_____

7. What was your first fight about

_____

8. What was the first holiday you spent together

_____

9. What was your first pet as a couple

_____

10. If you don't have kids yet and you plan to, what would you like to name your first child: name for both a boy and a girl

_____

_____

5

Do You Remember

1. How old was he when you got married

_____

2. What time of the day/night did you get married

_____

3. Was he named after someone

_____

4. A nickname he had when growing up

_____

5. A story of his childhood he told you about

_____

6. As a child, what (career) did he want to be when he grew up

_____

7. A memorable event in his life he told you about

_____

_____

8. What was the scariest thing that ever happened to him

_____

_____

_____

9. What was the most embarrasing thing that ever happened to him

_____

_____

10. A struggle he overcame or went through in life that he confided in you about

_____

_____

_____

6

Romance

1. My first impression of him was

_____

2. How old was he when you met

_____

3. On your first date did he:

    A. foul

    B. strike out

    C. get to first base

    D. hit a home run

4. What was it about him that first drew him to you

_____

_____

5. Name something you always did before you went out on a date, that you no longer do

_____

6. How long did you date before you saw each other exclusively

_____

7. How long after you knew him before you knew, "He was the one!"

_____

8. To me a perfect date with him would be

_____

_____

9. What "sold" you on making a lasting relationship with him

_____

10. If a song was written about us, what would be the name of the song

_____

7

Wedding, Honeymoon & A New Life

1. Who proposed & how

_____

_____

_____

2. Use one word to describe him on your wedding day

_____

3. Name a song played at your wedding (the song you first danced to as husband and wife)

_____

4. Who was his best man: your maid of honor

_____

_____

5. Who caught the bridal bouquet/garter

_____

_____

6. What was the most memorable thing that happened on your honeymoon

_____

_____

7. Who chose the place where you spent your honeymoon

_____

8. Your first address as a couple

_____

9. How long have you been married

_____

10. How did you celebrate your first anniversary

_____

_____

8

Favorites

1. What is your favorite body part of his

_____

2. What is his favorite TV show

_____

3. What is his favorite movie

_____

4. What is his favorite way to spend "free" time

_____

5. What is your favorite thing he does to make you feel special

_____

_____

_____

9

How Observant Are You

1. What kind of cologne does he wear

_____

2. Without looking: What is he wearing now

_____

3. What month did you meet

_____

4. What is the color of his toothbrush

_____

5. What is the color of his favorite shirt

_____

10

Relationships

1. Which video game best describes your relationship:

   A. Final Fantasy

   B. Sims

   C. Nintendogs

   D. Call of Duty

   E. Need For Speed

   F. No idea, we don't play video games. Then make up a name of a video game that would best describe your life/relationship

   _____

2. Which one of his friends would he be least likely to share a secret with

   _____

3. Does he spend more time looking at the screen of his smartphone or at you

   _____

4. If one of you was a Democrat and the other a Republican or a Libertarian: would that affect your relationship. How would you solve the issue

_____

5. Which TV show best describes your relationship:

A. Ozzie & Harriet

B. Friends

C. Everybody Loves Raymond

D. Battlestar Gallactica

E. Parenthood

F. The Brady Bunch

6. What is the best advice he has ever given you

_____

_____

7. What would you do if you saw someone flirting with him

A get angry and tell her he belongs to you

B smile and walk up and introduce yourself

C get angry and want to leave

D just have a good time and know you can trust him and he will handle the situation himself

E Fill in your own answer

_____

8. What would you do if a friend called you and told you she had seen your loved one out to lunch with another woman and they looked pretty cozy. How would you respond

_____

_____

9. What is the most embarrasing thing he did in front of your family and friends

_____

_____

10. Write the first thing that comes to mind: I am so appreciative of him because

_____

_____

_____

11

Friendships

1. Who makes friends easier: you or your loved one

_____

2. Do you get along with his friends

_____

3. Does he like or get along with your best friend

_____

4. Does he have a friend that you're not really crazy about and if so who is it

_____

5. What friend does he have that you both know you can rely on when you really need someone

_____

12

Other Family Members

1. What was your first impression of your in-laws

_____

2. Did your in-laws welcome you into the family with love and open arms or was it a battle

_____

3. Would you rather have a relationship like his parents or your parents and why

_____

_____

4. What do you admire the most about his mother

_____

5. What do you admire the most about his father

_____

6. What was your initial thought when you met his parents

_____

7. What are his grandparent's first names (either maternal or paternal)

_____

_____

8. What is his mother's maiden name

_____

9. Using your parents or his parent's marriage as an example; what do you admire in their marriage that you would like to copy in your own relationship

_____

_____

_____

10. Were his grandparents a large part of his life growing up

_____

13

Holidays

1. What was his favorite holiday as a child

_____

2. What is his favorite holiday now

_____

3. How do you make his birthday a special day for him

_____

_____

4. What traditions (concerning holidays) did he have as a child that you would like to continue with your own family

_____

_____

5. What new holiday traditions would you like to start in your family

_____

_____

6. What was different about how he celebrated certain holidays than you did while growing up

_____

_____

7. During the holidays what does he most look forward to

_____

8. During the holidays what does he least look forward to

_____

_____

9. What can you do to change the answer above so he enjoys the holidays as much as you do

_____

_____

10. What is his favorite time of year to take a vacation

_____

14

Food

1. Late at night, what is he most likely to snack on

_____

2. If you served him _____, he would most likely push it to the side of the plate and not eat it.

3. Name a food he eats you would NEVER eat

_____

4. My favorite dish he cooks for me is

_____

5. What recipe that his mother used to make for him when he was growing up does he brag about the most

_____

Hint: Ask her for the recipe and let her know how much he enjoyed it. You will make both his mother and him happy by doing so.

15

Which One Is...

1. Is he an early bird or a night owl; which are you

_____

2. Who is most often late of the two of you

_____

3. Who is most likely to "misplace" their keys, phone, forget about an event...

_____

4. Which of the two of you is most likely to instigate sex

_____

5. While you are out to dinner or out with friends, of the two of you which one is most likely to be the first to check their phone for messages

_____

16

Finish This Sentence

1. The first thing he does in the morning is

_____

2. He drives me crazy when

_____

_____

3. How would you complete these sentences: I hate to be

_____

He hates to be

_____

4. How would you complete these sentences: I am scared of

_____

He is scared of

5. How do you think he would complete this sentence: If I could change anything about myself, I would change

_____

6. I wish he wouldn't

_____

7. I love it when he

_____

8. When I smell

_____

I think of you

9. He makes me feel special when he brags about my

_____

10. When the charge card bill comes in the mail and you see how much he spent for a nonessential item he "just had to have" that doesn't really fit in the budget and you see how much it really cost, do you:

A. Ask him to return it

B. Ask him what he was thinking

C. Say OK, now I can get the _____I really wanted

D. Just say it's ok; he really deserves to splurge on himself a little bit whether it fits in the budget or not

17

It's All About Him

1. What kind of animal does he most remind you of:

   A. wild stallion

   B. teddy bear

   C. pig

   D. myna bird

   E. lemming

   F. sloth

2. I think his most admirable trait is

   _____

3. He hates it when I

   _____

4. If he was a super hero, what would his super hero powers be

   _____

5. What super hero does he most remind you of

_____

6. If he was a super hero, what would his super hero name be

_____

7. What is his favorite color

_____

8. What is his dream car

_____

9. Last week he brought you home some beautiful flowers just because he loves you, what special gift could you bring him just because you love him

_____

10. In what way do you wish you could be more like him

_____

_____

18

Entertainment

1. What is his favorite book

_____

2. What is his favorite type of music

_____

3. What is his favorite place to go to hang out with friends

_____

4. What is his favorite movie star

_____

5. What is his favorite sport

_____

19

How Well Do You *REALLY* Know Your Mate

1. If he won the lottery what is the first thing he would purchase

_____

2. They say men marry women like their mother: How are you similar to his mother

_____

3. If he were stranded on a desert island, name one thing he would wish he could have on the island with him – besides you

_____

4. What is the first car he owned

_____

5. If he could have plastic surgery; what body part would he most like to change

_____

6. If he could choose any job – what would be his dream job

_____

7. Name a person in history he admires

_____

8. What is his favorite season of the year

_____

9. If he could choose any time era to live in; what time era do you think it would be and why

_____

_____

10. Name someone who has been an inspiration to him

_____

_____

20

Do You Agree

1. Who is the funniest of the two of you

_____

2. Who is the better driver of the two of you

_____

3. If he was given the choice to live anywhere in the world where would it be and do you feel the same way about moving there

_____

_____

4. If someone told him they were going to give the two of you a gift card for $1,000 and just tell them the name of the store he wanted it from, which store would he choose? Would you come up with the same store?

_____

_____

5. If you offered him his choice of restaurants to go out for dinner, what would he pick:

A. Italian

B. Mexican

C. Chinese / Thai / Sushi

D. Mediterranean

E. American: Burgers / BBQ/ Fried Chicken

21

Emotions

1. It brings a smile to my face everytime I think about the time he

_____

2. I really appreciate him for

_____

_____

3. I don't tell him enough, how much it means to me that he

_____

4. I catch myself laughing out loud everytime I think about

_____

5. It breaks my heart everytime I think about

_____

When You Don't Always See Eye To Eye

1. What is the one thing he has too much of

_____

2. If he could throw away one thing that belonged to you, what would it be

_____

3. What is the biggest thing you don't agree on

_____

_____

4. You're going out on date night, dinner and to a movie. He wants to see the latest adventure flick, you want to see a chick flick. Which movie would you most likely end up at

_____

5. You have just met a new couple that wants to hang out with you and your mate. You can't stand them, your mate thinks they're a lot of fun. What do you do

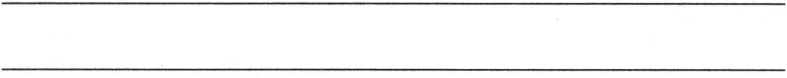

23

Character Flaws

1. Of the two of you, who has more of a tendency to think they're right all the time

_____

2. Does he forgive and forget or hold a grudge

_____

3. Who has to get in the last word in an argument

_____

4. Who is the most jealous of the two of you

_____

5. Who is the biggest spendthrift of the two of you

_____

24

Character Assets

1. Of the two of you, who is the bigger extrovert

_____

2. He always has a great outlook about

_____

3. After a fight, who makes the first gesture to make up

_____

4. What is his biggest asset

_____

5. When you don't feel well or are just plain tired, what kind gesture does he do to make you feel better

_____

_____

_____

25

Just For The Fun Of It

1. Remember the time we went

_____

and we laughed like kids and had such a great time. Let's make plans and do it again.

2. If you suggested a walk or a picnic where you could just hold hands and spend time just the two of you, do you think he would:

   A. agree; make plans to do so thinking it was a great idea

   B. make excuses

   C. put you off for another time

   D. flat out refuse; saying it wasn't his kind of thing

3. How would you pass the time if you lost the electricity for an evening

_____

4. You have your choice, for the two of you, would you rather spend a weekend:

A at a theme park

B at a national park

C a weekend away at a hotel, dancing, dinner out

D getting things caught up around the house

E gambling in Vegas

5. You had planned for a quiet romantic weekend. You made his favorite dinner, lit candles around the house, with rose petals leading to the bedroom. You just took dinner out of the oven and are expecting him to come in the door any minute, but when he comes in he's excited and doesn't notice the romantic music, candles, and his favorite dinner or the rose petals. He wraps you in a hug in his arms and tells you his best friend just offered him tickets on the 50 yard line at the Super Bowl and it's his favorite team playing. But, if he's going to go he has to pack and leave in the next 15 minutes. How do you react:

A. You're happy he has this opportunity to go see his favorite team at such an important event and tell him to get a shower and you'll pack for him

B. Tell him of your own plans for the weekend for the two of you

C. Tell him to go if he wants, but you're *not happy!*

Social Media

1. In this day of social media where it consumes so much of our time and attention; what can you do to not let it become a problem in your relationship

_____

2. Would you post a photo on Facebook, Instagram, or Snapchat that you know he wouldn't be happy about if he found out what you did

A. Yes

B. No

C. Depends on what it was

3. Did you ever tweet a message out of anger that you wish you hadn't

A. Yes

B. No

4. Have you ever googled his past girlfriend

A. Yes

B. No

5. When you need to contact him throughout the day, do you more often than not:

A. call him so you can hear his voice and connect with him

B. email

C. text

D. Fill in your own blank_____

27

This Is What I *REALLY* Love About Him

1. What was it about him that attracted you to him in the first place

_____

2. What is it about him that made you want him in your life

_____

3. What is something he does for you that makes you feel loved and special

_____

4. Name something you REALLY appreciate about him

_____

5. I love to watch him when he doesn't know it and this is what I see

_____

28

I'll Never Forget The Time

1. I'll never forget the time we

_____

2. Our worst vacation and why

_____

3. The most special time in our life so far was when

_____

4. He really surprised me when

_____

5. Something really special a friend did for us that meant a lot to both of us was when

_____

6. At the time _____

happened I didn't think it was funny, but now I can look back and laugh about it

7. I'll never forget the day/night we met when he

_____

8. After our marriage vows when we were pronounced man and wife, I looked at you and

_____

9. I was so embarrassed when

_____

10. The first time you said I love you my immediate reaction was

_____

29

Test Your Memory

1. What is his most overused expression

_____

2. What is the first meal he ever cooked for you

_____

3. What was your first address together

_____

4. What is the last thing he said to "remind me..."

_____

5. Give his routine of when he walks in the door, in the order of how he does things. OR The order of things he does when he gets up in the morning: your choice: (Ex.: throw keys on table, sit in favorite chair, kick off his shoes, ask what's for dinner....)

1.

2.

3.

4.

30

Religion

1. What Bible verse do you use as inspiration in your relationship

_____

2. If the two of you could do one thing to help someone in a way that would make a major impact on someone else's life – what would it be

_____

3. Is your faith important to you? Is his faith important to him?

_____

4. What is a Bible verse that helps to get him through tough times

_____

5. When he thinks of church, does he

A Think it's ok for other people if that's what they're into

B Get encouragement from going and hope he gives encouragement to others

C Think it's a place just to go for weddings and funerals

D Something he would like to look into

E Something he might consider when you have kids

31

Regrets

1. What is one thing he's regretted more than anything else

_____

_____

2. If there is one piece of advice someone gave him that he now wishes he would have listened to, what was it

_____

_____

3. The Bible says: "Don't let the sun go down on your anger." You were really angry at him and made him sleep on the couch and didn't speak to him before you left for work. You know anger between you isn't a good thing. If you could sit down together and remedy this issue what would you say

_____

_____

4. If there is one thing you said or did in your relationship

you wish you could take back, what is it

_____

5. In your obituary, how will you be remembered:

Did you live the sort of life that others will remember you
fondly and will be missed, *or not*. Age isn't an indicator of
how long we live. We can walk out the door tomorrow and
be killed in a car accident or have a heart attack; is there
anything you need to change in your life to be a better
person, and if so what changes would you like to make or
what aspects in your character do you need to work on

_____

_____

_____

32

Think About It

1. What one characteristic in a person annoys him the most

_____

2. What can I do today to make it a better day for the love of my life

_____

_____

3. When I talk I feel he really listens to what I'm saying.

   True or False

4. When you call him and he answers "Just a minute," what does that mean to you

_____

5. What is the strangest gift he has ever given you

_____

33

What Would You Do

1. Your house is on fire: you have saved all family members and pets. What is the one other thing you would save if you had time to get one more thing?

_____

2. If you found a $100 bill; what would you spend it on

_____

3. You have just finished building a time machine and you know it works. You grab your mate and buckle yourselves in. To what event in history would you go to experience for yourselves

_____

4. You know a friend, or know of a stranger or friend of a friend, who is suffering hard times. What thing would you most like to do to help this person or family (within reason, something not out of the realm of reality)

_____

5. You are at a family reunion and someone has just told everyone a story about your loved one that you know embarrasses him, what do you do

_____

34

Random Thoughts & Questions

1. What celebrity does your mate most resemble

_____

2. If he went and had his hair cut and he really likes it but you don't; how would you respond when he asks what you think about it

_____

3. What blood type does he have

_____

4. If he just learned he had 24 hours to live, how would he spend that time

_____

_____

5 What would he pick as his last meal

_____

6. Name one thing he would have on his bucket list

_____

7. What is the nicest thing someone else ever did for him

_____

8. Does he have any medical allergies or a medical history you need to know about for the future

_____

9. Name one event in his life that left a large impact on his life, character, or attitude

_____

10. What are your goals for this year as a couple

_____

_____

_____

_____

Now It's His Turn

The following pages are for the man in your life to fill in

1

In The Beginning

1. What is the name of the hospital where she was born

_____

2. How much did she weigh when she was born

_____

3. Was she born in the morning or the evening

_____

4. In what city was she born

_____

5. What is her birthdate – including the year

_____

6. What day of the week was she born

_____

7. What is her middle name

_____

8. What was her favorite toy as a child

_____

9. Did you grow up in the same city and state she did

_____

10. What is her astrological sign

_____

2

School Days

1. What do you remember of a school memory she told you about

_____

_____

2. Where did she attend elementary school

_____

3. What was her favorite subject in school

_____

4. What was her least favorite subject

_____

5. Where did she attend high school...name of school

_____

6. What was her major in college

_____

7. What is the most embarrassing thing she did in her school days

_____

_____

8. Was there a teacher that inspired or influenced her in any way

_____

9. Her most memorable teacher (good or bad) was

_____

10. She went to college with the intention of pursuing what career

_____

3

When You Met

1. How did you meet each other:

   A. work

   B. through a friend

   C. social media

   D. out and about / intrduced ourselves

2. Where did you meet

   _____

3. What was your first impression of her

   _____

4. What did you find you had in common when you first met

   _____

5. Do you remember what you talked about the first time

you met

_____

6. If she asked you for your phone number/text/email
address/ to friend you on facebook; what was your first
thought:

   A. give her the info

   B. give her a wrong number/email address

   C. hope she would contact you ASAP

7. Did you initially hope she would contact you again after
the first day/night you met

_____

8. What was the first positive trait about her that made you
think perhaps this was meant to be

_____

9. After your friends met her, what was their advice to you

_____

10. After your parents met her, what was their advice to
you

_____

4

First Time For Everything

1. Where did you go on your first date?

_____

2. Where were you when you first kissed?

_____

3. Who called/texted/ or emailed who first

_____

4 Who said I love you first?

_____

5. What is the first gift she bought for you?

_____

6. How long did you know her before you first met her family

7. What was your first fight about

_____

8. What was the first holiday you spent together

_____

9. What was your first pet as a couple

_____

10. If you don't have kids yet and you plan to, what would you like to name your first child: name for both a boy and a girl

_____

_____

5

Do You Remember

1. How old was she when you got married

_____

2. What time of the day/night did you get married

_____

3. Was she named after someone

_____

4. A nickname she had when growing up

_____

5. A story of her childhood she told you about

_____

6. As a child, what (career) did she want to be when she grew up

_____

7. A memorable event in her life she told you about

_____

_____

8. What was the scariest thing that ever happened to her

_____

_____

_____

9. What was the most embarrasing thing that ever happened to her

_____

_____

10. A struggle she overcame or went through in life that she confided in you about

_____

_____

_____

6

Romance

1. My first impression of her was

_____

2. How old was she when you met

_____

3. On your first date did you:

    A. foul

    B. strike out

    C. get to first base

    D. hit a home run

4. What was it about her that first drew her to you

_____

_____

5. Name something you always did before you went out on

a date, that you no longer do

_____

6. How long did you date before you saw each other exclusively

_____

7. How long after you knew her before you knew, "She was the one!"

_____

8. To me a perfect date with her would be

_____

_____

9. What "sold" you on making a lasting relationship with her

_____

10. If a song was written about us, what would be the name of the song

_____

7

Wedding, Honeymoon & A New Life

1. Who proposed & how

_____

_____

_____

2. Use one word to describe her on your wedding day

_____

3. Name a song played at your wedding (the song you first danced to as husband and wife)

_____

4. Who was your best man: her maid of honor

_____

_____

5. Who caught the bridal bouquet/garter

_____

_____

6. What was the most memorable thing that happened on your honeymoon

_____

_____

7. Who chose the place where you spent your honeymoon

_____

8. Your first address as a couple

_____

9. How long have you been married

_____

10. How did you celebrate your first anniversary

_____

_____

8

Favorites

1. What is your favorite body part of hers

_____

2. What is her favorite TV show

_____

3. What is her favorite movie

_____

4. What is her favorite way to spend "free" time

_____

5. What is your favorite thing she does to make you feel special

_____

_____

_____

9

How Observant Are You

1. What kind of perfume does she wear

_____

2. Without looking: What is she wearing now

_____

3. What month did you meet

_____

4. What is the color of her toothbrush

_____

5. What is the color of her favorite top

_____

10

Relationships

1. Which video game best describes your relationship:

A. Final Fantasy

B. Sims

C. Nintendogs

D. Call of Duty

E. Need For Speed

F. No idea, we don't play video games. Then make up a name of a video game that would best describe your life/relationship

_____

2. Which one of her friends would she be least likely to share a secret with

_____

3. Does she spend more time looking at the screen of her smartphone or at you

_____

4. If one of you was a Democrat and the other a Republican or a Libertarian: would that affect your relationship. How would you solve the issue

_____

5. Which TV show best describes your relationship:

   A. Ozzie & Harriet

   B. Friends

   C. Everybody Loves Raymond

   D. Battlestar Gallactica

   E. Parenthood

   F. The Brady Bunch

6. What is the best advice she has ever given you

_____

_____

7. What would you do if you saw someone flirting with her

   A get angry and tell him she belongs to you

   B smile and walk up and introduce yourself

   C get angry and want to leave

   D just have a good time and know you can trust her and she will handle the situation herself

E Fill in your own answer

_____

8. What would you do if a friend called you and told you he had seen your loved one out to lunch with another man and they looked pretty cozy. How would you respond

_____

_____

9. What is the most embarrasing thing she ever did in front of your family and friends

_____

_____

10. Write the first thing that comes to mind: I am so appreciative of her because

_____

_____

_____

11

Friendships

1. Who makes friends easier: you or your loved one

_____

2. Do you get along with her friends

_____

3. Does she like or get along with your best friend

_____

4. Does she have a friend that you're not really crazy about and if so who is it

_____

5. What friend does she have that you both know you can rely on when you really need someone

_____

12

Other Family Members

1. What was your first impression of your in-laws

_____

2. Did your in-laws welcome you into the family with love and open arms or was it a battle

_____

3. Would you rather have a relationship like her parents or your parents and why

_____

_____

4. What do you admire the most about her mother

_____

5. What do you admire the most about her father

_____

6. What was your initial thought when you met her parents

_____

7. What are her grandparent's first names (either maternal or paternal)

_____

_____

8. What is her mother's maiden name

_____

9. Using your parents or her parent's marriage as an example; what do you admire in their marriage that you would like to copy in your own relationship

_____

_____

_____

10. Were her grandparents a large part of her life growing up

_____

13

Holidays

1. What was her favorite holiday as a child

_____

2. What is her favorite holiday now

_____

3. How do you make her birthday a special day for her

_____

_____

4. What traditions (concerning holidays) did she have as a child that you would like to continue with your own family

_____

_____

5. What new holiday traditions would you like to start in your family

_____

_____

6. What was different about how she celebrated certain holidays than you did while growing up

_____

_____

7. During the holidays what does she most look forward to

_____

8. During the holidays what does she least look forward to

_____

_____

9. What can you do to change the answer above so she enjoys the holidays as much as you do

_____

_____

10. What is her favorite time of year to take a vacation

_____

14

Food

1. Late at night, what is she most likely to snack on

_____

2. If you served her _____, she would most likely push it to the side of the plate and not eat it.

3. Name a food she eats you would NEVER eat

_____

4. My favorite dish she cooks for me is

_____

5. What recipe that her mother used to make for her when she was growing up does she brag about the most

_____

15

Which One Is...

1. Is she an early bird or a night owl

_____

2. Who is most often late of the two of you

_____

3. Who is most likely to "misplace" their keys, phone, forget about an event...

_____

4. Which of the two of you is most likely to instigate sex

_____

5. While you are out to dinner or out with friends, of the two of you which one is most likely to be the first to check their phone for messages

_____

16

Finish This Sentence

1. The first thing she does in the morning is

_____

2. She drives me crazy when

_____

_____

3. How would you complete these sentences: I hate to be

_____

She hates to be

_____

4. How would you complete these sentences: I am scared of

_____

She is scared of

5. How do you think she would complete this sentence: If I could change anything about myself, I would change

_____

6. I wish she wouldn't

_____

7. I love it when she

_____

8. When I smell

_____

I think of you

9. She makes me feel special when she brags about my

_____

10. When the charge card bill comes in the mail and you see how much she spent for a nonessential item she "just had to have" that doesn't really fit in the budget and you see how much it really cost, do you:

A. Ask her to return it

B. Ask her what she was thinking

C. Say OK, now I can get the _____I really wanted

D. Just say it's ok; she really deserves to splurge on herself a little bit whether it fits in the budget or not

17

It's All About Her

1. What kind of animal does she most remind you of:

   A. kitten

   B. K-9 dog

   C. pig

   D. lemming

   E. lamb

   F. racehorse

2. I think her most admirable trait is

   _____

3. She hates it when I

   _____

4. If she was a super hero, what would her super hero powers be

   _____

5. What super hero does she most remind you of

_____

6. If she was a super hero, what would her super hero name be

_____

7. What is her favorite color

_____

8. What are her favorite flowers

_____

9. When is the last time you bought her flowers and it wasn't a holiday

_____

10. In what way do you wish you could be more like her

_____

_____

18

Entertainment

1. What is her favorite book

_____

2. What is her favorite type of music

_____

3. What is her favorite place to go to hang out with friends

_____

4. What is her favorite movie star

_____

5. What is her favorite sport

_____

19

How Well Do You *REALLY* Know Your Mate

1. If she won the lottery what is the first thing she would purchase

_____

2. They say women marry men similar to their father: How are you similar to her father

_____

3. If she were stranded on a desert island, name one thing she would wish she could have on the island with her – besides you

_____

4. What is the first car she owned

_____

5. If she could have plastic surgery; what body part would she most like to change

_____

6. If she could choose any job – what would be her dream
job

_____

7. Name a person in history she admires

_____

8. What is her favorite season of the year

_____

9. If she could choose any time era to live in; what time era
do you think it would be and why

_____

_____

10. Name someone who has been an inspiration to her

_____

_____

20

Do You Agree

1. Who is the funniest of the two of you

_____

2. Who is the better driver of the two of you

_____

3. If she was given the choice to live anywhere in the world where would it be and do you feel the same way about moving there

_____

_____

4. If someone told her they were going to give the two of you a gift card for $1,000 and just tell them the name of the store she wanted it from, which store would she choose? Would you come up with the same store?

_____

_____

5. If you offered her a choice of restaurants to go out to, what would she pick:

A. Italian

B. Mexican

C. Chinese / Thai / Sushi

D. Mediterranean

E. American: Burgers / BBQ/ Fried Chicken

21

Emotions

1. It brings a smile to my face everytime I think about the time she

_____

2. I really appreciate her for

_____

_____

3. I don't tell her enough, how much it means to me that she

_____

4. I catch myself laughing out loud everytime I think about

_____

5. It breaks my heart everytime I think about

_____

When You Don't Always See Eye To Eye

1. What is the one thing she has too much of

_____

2. If she could throw away one thing that belonged to you, what would it be

_____

3. What is the biggest thing you don't agree on

_____

_____

4. You're going out on date night, dinner and to a movie. You want to see the latest adventure flick, she wants to see a chick flick. Which movie would you most likely end up at

_____

5. You have just met a new couple that wants to hang out with you and your mate. You can't stand them, your mate thinks they're a lot of fun. What do you do

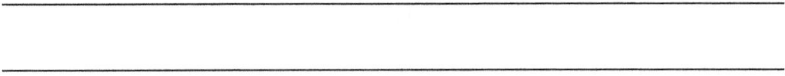

23

Character Flaws

1. Of the two of you, who has more of a tendency to think they're right all the time

_____

2. Does she forgive and forget or hold a grudge

_____

3. Who has to get in the last word in an argument

_____

4. Who is the most jealous of the two of you

_____

5. Who is the biggest spendthrift of the two of you

_____

24

Character Assets

1. Of the two of you, who is the bigger extrovert

_____

2. She always has a great outlook about

_____

3. After a fight, who makes the first gesture to make up

_____

4. What is her biggest asset

_____

5. When you don't feel well or are just plain tired, what kind gesture does she do to make you feel better

_____

_____

_____

25

Just For The Fun Of It

1. Remember the time we went

_____

and we laughed like kids and had such a great time. Let's make plans and do it again.

2. If you suggested going to a car show, do you think she would:

   A. agree; and make plans to do so

   B. make excuses

   C. put you off for another time

   D. flat out refuse; saying it wasn't her kind of thing

3. How would you pass the time if you lost the electricity for an evening

_____

4. You have your choice, for the two of you, would you rather spend a weekend:

A at a theme park

B at a national park

C a weekend away at a hotel, dancing, dinner out

D getting things caught up around the house

E gambling in Vegas

5. Your best friend has called with tickets for the Super Bowl where your favorite team is playing. You have to pack and meet him at the airport in an hour which gives you time to get home and get packed and leave within 10 – 15 minutes. You rush in the door excited with your news wondering if she will be OK with you going off for the weekend as she hinted on the phone she had plans herself for the two of you this weekend. When you walk in you notice she made your favorite dinner, the romantic candles and music playing and rose petals leading to the bedroom. How do you react:

A You kiss her and say how excited you are about the weekend she has planned and quietly go phone your friend and tell him you can't make it after all

B Tell her your news and thank her for all she's done and tell her you'll make it up to her with your own romantic plans next weekend and tell her to go shopping and splurge on something for herself over the weekend

C You go even though she's upset and leave the house where you are both mad at each other

26

Social Media

1. In this day of social media where it consumes so much of our time and attention; what can you do to not let it become a problem in your relationship

_____

2. Would you post a photo on Facebook, Instagram, or Snapchat that you know she wouldn't be happy about if she found out what you did

    A. Yes

    B. No

    C. Depends on what it was

3. Did you ever tweet a message out of anger that you wish you hadn't

    A. Yes

    B. No

4. Have you ever googled her past boyfriend

    A. Yes

B. No

5. When you need to contact her throughout the day, do you more often than not:

A. call her so you can hear her voice and connect with her

B. email

C. text

D. Fill in your own blank_____

27

This Is What I *REALLY* Love About Her

1. What was it about her that attracted you to her in the first place

_____

2. What is it about her that made you want her in your life

_____

3. What is something she does for you that makes you feel loved and special

_____

4. Name something you *REALLY* appreciate about her

_____

5. I love to watch her when she doesn't know it and this is what I see

_____

28

I'll Never Forget The Time

1. I'll never forget the time we

_____

2. Our worst vacation and why

_____

3. The most special time in our life so far was when

_____

4. She really surprised me when

_____

5. Something really special a friend did for us that meant a lot to both of us was when

_____

6. At the time _____

happened I didn't think it was funny, but now I can look back and laugh about it

7. I'll never forget the day/night we met when she

_____

8. After our marriage vows when we were pronounced man and wife, I looked at you and

_____

9. I was so embarrassed when

_____

10. The first time you said I love you my immediate reaction was

_____

29

Test Your Memory

1. What is her most overused expression

_____

2. What is the first meal she ever cooked for you

_____

3. What was your first address together

_____

4. What is the last thing she said to "remind me..."

_____

5. Give her routine of when she walks in the door, in the order of how she does things. OR The order of things she does when she gets up in the morning: your choice: (Ex.: throw keys on table, sit in favorite chair, kick off her shoes, ask you to call to have a pizza delivered....)

1.

2.

3.

4.

30

Religion

1. What Bible verse do you use as inspiration in your relationship

_____

2. If the two of you could do one thing to help someone in a way that would make a major impact on someone else's life – what would it be

_____

3. Is your faith important to you? Is her faith important to her?

_____

4. What is a Bible verse that helps to get her through tough times

_____

5. When she thinks of church, does she

   A Think it's ok for other people if that's what they're into

B Get encouragement from going and hope she gives encouragement to others

C Think it's a place just to go for weddings and funerals

D Something she would like to look into

E Something she might consider when you have kids

31

Regrets

1. What is one thing she's regretted more than anything else

_____

_____

2. If there is one piece of advice someone gave her that she now wishes she would have listened to, what was it

_____

_____

3. The Bible says: "Don't let the sun go down on your anger." You were really angry at her and slept on the couch and didn't speak to her before you left for work. You know anger between you isn't a good thing. If you could sit down together and remedy this issue what would you say

_____

_____

4. If there is one thing you said or did in your relationship you wish you could take back, what is it

_____

5. In your obituary, how will you be remembered:

Did you live the sort of life that others will remember you fondly and will be missed, *or not*. Age isn't an indicator of how long we live. We can walk out the door tomorrow and be killed in a car accident or have a heart attack; is there anything you need to change in your life to be a better person and if so what changes would you like to make or what aspects in your character do you need to work on

_____

_____

_____

32

Think About It

1. What one characteristic in a person annoys her the most

_____

2. What can I do today to make it a better day for the love of my life

_____

_____

3. When I talk I feel she really listens to what I'm saying.

   True   or   False

4. When you call her and she answers "Just a minute," what does that mean to you

_____

5. What is the strangest gift she has ever given you

_____

33

What Would You Do

1. Your house is on fire: you have saved all family members and pets. What is the one other thing you would save if you had time to get one more thing?

_____

2. If you found a $100 bill; what would you spend it on

_____

3. You have just finished building a time machine and you know it works. You grab your mate and buckle yourselves in. To what event in history would you go to experience for yourselves

_____

4. You know a friend, or know of a stranger or friend of a friend, who is suffering hard times. What thing would you most like to do to help this person or family (within reason, something not out of the realm of reality)

_____

5. You are at a family reunion and someone has just told everyone a story about your loved one that you know embarrasses her, what do you do

---

34

Random Thoughts & Questions

1. What celebrity does your mate most resemble

_____

2. If she went and had her hair cut and styled and she really likes it but you don't; how would you respond when she asks what you think about it

_____

3. What blood type does she have

_____

4. If she just learned she has 24 hours to live, how would she spend that time

_____

_____

5 What would she pick as her last meal

_____

6. Name one thing she would have on her bucket list

_____

7. What is the nicest thing someone else ever did for her

_____

8. Does she have any medical allergies or a medical history you need to know about for the future

_____

9. Name one event in her life that left a large impact on her life, character, or attitude

_____

10. What are your goals for this year as a couple

_____

_____

_____

_____

I HOPE YOU HAD A GOOD TIME FILLING THIS
OUT AND HAD SOME QUALITY TIME TOGETHER
WHILE DOING SO AND MAYBE EVEN LEARNED A
LITTLE BIT ABOUT EACH OTHER.

www.ingramcontent.com/pod-product-compliance
Lightning Source LLC
Chambersburg PA
CBHW060308050426
42448CB00009B/1762